# Aai's Malvani Diary

Pinakin Sabnis

 pencil

ISBN 978-93-5610-719-9
© Pinakin Sabnis 2022
Published in India 2022 by Pencil

*A brand of*
One Point Six Technologies Pvt. Ltd.
123, Building J2, Shram Seva Premises,
Wadala Truck Terminal, Wadala (E)
Mumbai 400037, Maharashtra, INDIA
**E** connect@thepencilapp.com
**W** www.thepencilapp.com

# Author biography

Hello Readers! Namaste. My name is Pinakin Sabnis. A typical Mumbaiya guy living with a lovely family. I work for a Private limited firm as a Market researcher full time. I own a blog called "Pinakin's Broadway", make sure you visit it. My hobbies cooking, cooking and only cooking. Yes, sleeping is a part of my hobby as well. My friends called me Snorlax (a pokemon) who too loves to eat and sleep. I love to travel as well but I am not a regular traveller. Twice or Thrice a year I visit places. But when I do I ensure I take a long vacation and enjoy every bit of that destination.

I am a total foodie. I love to explore food from various cuisines. Till now I have tasted Continental, Indian (North, South, West and little bit of East), Indo-Chinese food (my favourite is Triple Rice). Not a big fan of sweets but I don't mind eating. Gulabjamun and Jaleebi are my favorites. I cook as well. My mother is a big critic of my food. The day she gives thumbs up to what I cook is what I post on my blog. My wife too cooks good food. She hails from Madhya Pradesh and I just love the Dal they make. Whenever I visit her place I tell them I am ok with Dal, Rice and Dry Chilli Teecha for my entire stay.

The art of cooking food in me came from my father. He was truely a good teacher. I still remember his Dal Fry, Tomato Alo mix vegetable and Jeera Rice he use to cook. Wow! it was heaven. He taught me several dishes including Dal Fry, Kheema, Sukka Chicken and Prawns Curry in Malvani style. He use to say, "Cook food with love and it would love you back." Miss you Dad! I would say I am lucky to get to taste food from various state. My mother cooks South style food (Karnataka), my wife (MP) and Goan food cooked by me.

Aai's Malvani Diary is dedicated to my family and all the coffee beans who helped me stay awake and made this book a dream of mine fulfilled. In this book I would be posting recipes from Malvan alongwith the history of the cuisine. I hope you enjoy reading and cooking.

Also, please dont forget to visit my blog for some mouth-watering recipes and travel related articles.

Read it, prepare it and please share me the feedback on my blog. Always remember, in life stay positive and be optimistic.

# CONTENTS

# Introduction

Aai's Malvani Diary is a recipe book straight from my mother's book. These recipes have been made by my Father and Mother. Each and every ingredients which they used, in proportion , the use of masalas etc are mentioned as per the way they used while cooking. I believe any food would taste excellent if cooked with love and Malvani food is no different.

Apart from recipe I would like my readers to know the history of Malvani Cuisine. I believe to know a cuisine you should know the roots of it, the history of it, the basic of recipes and cuisines etc. So readers, get ready to dive in the history of Malvan and cook the recipes mentioned in this cook book with love. Surprise your friends and family members with these wonderful recipes. My personal favourite is Sol Kadi and Komdi Vade, but I am sure you would love to taste everything mentioned in this book. Please do comment and let me know if you get a chance to cook these lovely recipes.

Do remember the mantra, "Cook with Love."

# The Malvan region and its wonderful cuisine Malvani Food

On the west coast of India lies the sprawling state of Maharashtra, with its varied and historic cuisine. In this state, just down to the south is the district of Sindhudurg and here is the town of Malvan, famous for its distinct regional Indian cuisine.

The Sindhudurg fort is the major attraction for tourists and in this beautiful historic town, tourists get to explore a regional cuisine known as Malvani cuisine. Being a salt belt, the word Mahalavan means rich in salt. Located from 500 km of the financial capital of India, Mumbai, this small town with its widespread coconut trees has many similarities with the kitchen and the culture of Indian food. Rice is of course the staple food and is generally enjoyed with ghee and curry. Buttermilk is a reality in every Malvani family, and the region's Indian spices are associated with tamarind and kokum, similar to konkan food. Vegetarians have a plethora of some delicious dishes, but the main attraction amongst foodies has been its seafood dishes and Malvani's non-vegetarian recipes.

# The golden history of Malvan region

Located in the Sindhudurg district of Maharashtra, Malvan is one of the state's most famous tourist attraction, with culturally authentic cuisine and the historical fabulous Sindhudurg Fort.

According to historical records, between the 6th and 7th centuries, the Chalukya ruled this region followed by Devgiri (10th century) and Vijaynagar (14th century). Adilshahi's reign began in the 15th century, followed by the reign of Chatrapatti Shivaji Maharaj's Maratha in the 16th century and British reign in the 17th century. Before the wayward Marathas breathed life into it, Malvan was a fishing village, one of many along the Konkan coast. In 1664, Chhatrapati Shivaji Maharaj set out to create Sindhudurg Fort on an island near Malvan. Medha and Dewoolwada were the two main areas in the town of Malvan. The surrounding land which was spread to about 3 kilometers long, was swampy and marshy. Dewoolwada was the end of the land, while Medha was an island.

Malvan had many salt pans. Some locals in this region claim that here in the past, salt were produced in significant amounts here in the past. The phrase "Lavan" is still used by salt producers, while "Mahalavan" refers to a place where salt was available in abundance. As a result, the name Malvan came into existence.

# The ABCs of Malvani Cuisine

Malvani cuisine dates back to the town of Malvan. This coastal town of Konkan has its own unique style of cuisine. Although Malvani food has its own independent identity, but on a deep down you will find, it slightly resembles to the cuisines from Maharashtra, Goa, and northern parts of West Karnataka.

The cuisine of the Malvani Coast offers an excellent variety of fish, poultry, and vegetable dishes, but shellfish and chicken are always in the limelight when it comes to Malvani dinner. The sole reason of the Malvani delicacies which makes it stand from rest of the cuisines across India is, it combines the spiciness of the masala with a hint of vinegary pungency from the Goan cuisine, the use of freshly grated coconut originating from the Karwar belt and the sweet and sour blend of the Sarawat Goud community. In terms of ingredients and cooking methods, Malvani's cuisine is different from the rest of the country. Although Malvani food is mostly non-vegetarian, there are delicious vegetarian options as well. Instead of rice, they consume bhakri (made from rice flour). It is the Malvani corresponding of Maharashtrian jowar and chapati. Nevertheless, the food is not all hot and spicy.

Jhinga Fry is one of the most popular dish made with fried shrimp sprinkled with flour. Along the Konkan coast, Mori Masala or shark curry, is a popular meal as well. I would suggest you to try the Paplet (pomfret) cooked in traditional Malvani masala curry, when you visit Malvan.

# Key spices and features of Malvani food

Let me admit that Malvani seafood curries are spicy and peppery, but I bet, the dish would taste so delicious, that it will make you lick your fingers. Mackerel, crab, and shrimp, fried or cooked with coconut masala paste, are the all-time favourites. Most of the Malvani dishes are usually fried in a pan or on a simmering curry. Some dishes also make use of dried kokum, tamarind, and raw mango.

Malvani cuisine makes wide use of dried or grated coconut paste. Some recipes also make use of Coconut milk. It also makes use of substantial amount of dried chili peppers, coriander seeds, cardamom, ginger, kokum, tamarind, and garam masala spices. A blend of 15 to16 dried spices makes up Malvani masala, a powdered dried masala. This masala is coarsely powdered and stored in jars and used as needed. This Malvani masala brings everyday recipes to life with its flavor and aroma, good enough to lick the fingers.

Each dish is a culinary joy for foodies, thanks to its freshness. Ginger, for example, is freshly chopped. Coconut, green chillies and even coriander leaves are also fresh and organic, thus adding delicious flavour to Malvani food. The kitchen also offers a variety of options for vegans and non-vegetarians.

A Malvani dish is incomplete without Kokam Kadi. It helps cool the linings of the stomach and eases the digestion process. This pink coloured drink includes kokum fruit, coconut milk, ginger, salt, asafoetida and green chilly.

# Is Malvani food different or similar to Konkani Food

The Konkan Belt stretches from Thane in Maharashtra to Mangalore in Karnataka with attractive beaches and historical forts. With influences from Maharashtra, Goa and Karnataka, the region is famous for serving some of the most delicious cuisines in the country. Although non-vegetarian meals are more common in Konkani cuisine.

Both Malvani and Konkani cuisines depend heavily on seafood. Malvani cuisine makes use of many spices including red chili, coriander seeds, peppercorns, cumin, cardamom, ginger, garlic etc. Although Konkani cuisine includes the "Konkanastha Brahmin" style of cooking, it is mild, delicious and vegetarian.

Fundamentally, Konkani cuisine is prepared in one of two styles: Karwar or Malvani. With its abundant use of fresh coconut, the Karwar style of Konkan cuisine is heavily influenced by Kerala and Karnataka cuisine, while the Malvani food is similar to Goan or Maharashtrian cuisine.

Coconut is also frequently used in the Malvani style of cooking. The use of kokum, tamarind, and raw mango, on the other hand, sets it apart from the Karwar style of cooking. Malvani masala is a mixture of 15-16 coarsely ground spices that does not necessarily spice up foods.

| Malvani Name | Meaning of the name |
| --- | --- |
| Kombdi | Chicken |
| Kolambi/Kolbi | Prawns/Shrimp |
| Bhaat | Rice |
| Sukka | Dry Masala |
| Rassa | Curry/Gravy |
| Bhaji | Fried Vegetable |
| Amthi | Lentil curry |
| Usal | Legumes curry |
| Vade | Deep fried Indian bread |
| Bharli | Stuffed |
| Tikhlya/Tikhat | Spicy |
| Mohri | Baby Shark |
| Paplet | Pomfret |
| Bangda | Mackerel |

| Tisrya/Shimpli | Clams/Shell fish |
| --- | --- |
| Surmai | King Mackerel/King Fish |
| Mandeli | Anchovies |
| Rawas | Salmon |
| Bombeel | Bombay Duck |

# Recipes

# Non-Veg Recipes

# Chicken Sukka - Malvani style

Kombdi Sukka is a dry chicken dish from the Malvan region of Maharashtra, where authentic and traditional spices are used in its preparation with coconuts. The traditional Malvani kombdi sukka recipe is eaten with vade.

There are different types of Sukka chicken variations. Sukka basically means dry roast. Chicken or Kombdi (in Marathi) is roasted with masala. Equally popular but very different from its cousin Magalorean chicken Sukka. Then there is Kerala Chicken Sukka recipe which is again very different from Konkani Chicken Sukka. Since the masalas are different, the flavor varies greatly from region to region.

**Preparation time:** 10 minutes
**Cooking time:** 1 hour 10 minutes
**Serves:** 4

**Ingredients:**
**For Masala:**

- 1 tsp Oil

- 1 medium sliced Onions

- 6 crushed Garlic cloves

- 1" roughly chopped Ginger

- 1/2 cup grated Coconut

- 8 dry red Bedge chillies

- 3 tbsp Water, you can add more if required to make a smooth paste

**For Chicken:**

- 2 tbsp Oil

- 2 tbsp Water

- 1½ tsp. Malvani masala

- 1/2 tsp Turmeric powder

- 1 tsp Coriander powder

- Salt as per taste

- 1/2 kg Medium cut Chicken on bones

- 2 blades of Kokum. This needs to be soaked in 3 tbsp water for atleast 10 min

- 1/2 tsp grated jaggery

- 1 tbsp chopped Coriander leaves

- 1 tbsp Lemon juice

- Coriander leaves to garnish

**Steps to make Malvani Chicken Sukka:**

- Let's first make masala. Take a flat pan and then add onions along with ginger and garlic. Roast till onions turn soft.

- Then add grated coconut and dry red bedgi chillies. If you are not able to find Bedgi Mirchi in stores you can have any low heat chillies. Fry till coconut turns light brown in color. Do not burn it. Transfer it in a blender. Let the mixture cool after which blend it ina  smooth paste by adding water as required. Set it aside.

- Now let's make chicken. In a deep pan heat oil on a medium flame and add the prepared masala. Mix it well for about 1-2 minutes. Add water as required. Keep sauting till oil seperates.

- Later add Malvani masala, turmeric powder, coriander powder and salt. Mix it well.

- Add chicken and mix it well till masala coats. Cover with lid and let it cook for about 30 minutes or till chicken turns tender. Add Kokum, Kokum water, jaggery and coriander leaves. Mix it well.

- Let it simmer for about 10 more minutes. Add lemon juice and mix well.Garnish it with coriander leaves and serve it with Vade, rice or bhakris.

# Malvani Kolambi Rassa

24

Kolambi Rassa is a prawn curry that is another Malwan culinary masterpiece. It gets its distinct flavour from traditional Malvan masala and tastes best when served with steamed rice. Kolambi Rassa, or prawn curry, is made with Malvani masalas that have a ginger garlic paste aroma. Kolambi Rassa is enhanced with turmeric powder, red chilli powder, kokum, and dry grated coconut.

**Preparation time:**15 minutes
**Cooking time:**30 minutes
**Serves:**6

**Ingredients:**

- 1 kg. - shrimp

- 3 to 4 cloves - garlic, finely minced

- 1/4 tsp - turmeric powder

- 1 tsp - garam masala powder

- 2 cups - coconut milk

- A marble sized tamarind, soaked/2 to 3 petals of Kokum, soaked

- Chopped cilantro, to garnish

- Salt, to taste

- Oil, as required

**For Ground paste:**

- 3/4 cup - chopped onion

- 1/2 cup - grated coconut

- 1 - cinnamon

- 2 - green cardamom

- 3 - cloves

- 2 - dry red chillies (adjust according to taste)

- 1 tbsp - coriander seeds

- 1/2 tsp - fennel seeds

- 1/4 tsp - fenugreek seeds

- 1 tbsp - oil

**Steps to prepare:**

- Wash and pat dry the shrimp.

- Set aside to marinate with a pinch of salt.

- To make the ground paste, heat a tablespoon of oil and sauté the cinnamon, cardamom, cloves, red chilies, coriander seeds, fennel seeds, and fenugreek seeds until fragrant.

- Fry the onion and grated coconut over medium-low heat until light golden brown.

- Place aside to cool.

- Put everything in a grinder to make a paste once it has reached room temperature.

- In the same pan, heat a tablespoon of oil, then add the minced garlic and turmeric powder and sauté until the raw smell goes away.

- Fry for a minute after adding the ground mixture; add half a cup of water and cook until the oil separates.

- Mix in the shrimp, then the coconut milk, tamarind/kokam extract, salt, and garam masala powder.

- Cook for 5 to 6 minutes, covered, or until the shrimp turns pink and is fully cooked.

- Garnish with cilantro and serve with rice/chapattis.

# Surmai Curry (Kingfish Curry)

The Malvani Fish Curry is a traditional fish curry from Malvani cuisine that is cooked with coconut milk and freshly ground malvani masala. The king fish in the fish curry adds a delicious flavour to the curry. Serve the fish curry with steamed rice and pomfret fries.

We used freshly ground malvani masala in the Malvani fish curry, which is slowly stewed with sautéed onions and tomatoes in coconut milk. A few pieces of kokum are also added to the curry to add a sour element.

Serve the Malvani Fish Curry Recipe along with some Steamed rice, Fish Fry, Pickled onions by the side to make a delicious lunch or dinner. It's also a great weekend lunch or dinner option.

**Preparation time:**10 minutes
**Cooking time:**30 minutes
**Serves:**2

**Ingredients:**

**For the Fish Curry**

- 1 inch Ginger , finely chopped

- 4 cloves Garlic , finely chopped

- 1 Onion , finely chopped

- 2 Tomato , finely chopped

- 1/2 cup Coconut milk

- 1/4 cup Tamarind Water

- 1 sprig Curry leaves

- 1 teaspoon Mustard seeds (Rai/ Kadugu)

- 1 teaspoon Mustard oil or normal oil

- Salt , to taste

## To Marinade

- 2 King fish , cut into flat fillet

- 1 teaspoon Red Chilli powder

- 1/2 teaspoon Turmeric powder (Haldi)

- 1 teaspoon Cumin powder (Jeera)

- 1 teaspoon Coriander Powder (Dhania)

- 1 Lemon juice

- Salt , to taste

## For the Malvani Masala

- 1 teaspoon Coriander (Dhania) Seeds

- 1/2 teaspoon Cumin seeds (Jeera)

- 1 teaspoon Fennel seeds (Saunf)

- 1 inch Cinnamon Stick (Dalchini)

- 2 Cloves (Laung)

- 1 Bay leaf (tej patta)

- 1 pinch Nutmeg

- 1/2 teaspoon Whole Black Peppercorns

- 4 Dry Red Chillies

- 1 Star anise

## Steps to prepare:

- To begin making the Malvani Fish Curry Recipe, we will first thoroughly wash and drain the king fish. Combine the red chilli powder, turmeric, cumin powder, coriander powder, salt to taste, and lemon juice in a mixing bowl. Mix everything together and marinate the fish for at least 30 minutes.

## Making Malvani masala:

- Dry roast the coriander seeds, cumin seeds, fennel, cloves, cinnamon, cloves, bay leaf, star anise, and black peppercorns in a saucepan for at least 5 minutes, until well roasted.

- After that, grind all of the roasted ingredients, along with the dry red chilies and nutmeg, to make a smooth Malvani masala powder.

## Making Fish curry:

- Warm a kadai with mustard oil and allow the mustard seeds to sputter for a few seconds. Stir in the curry leaves.

- Allow it to crackle before adding the chopped ginger, garlic, and onions. Stir fry until the onions soften and turn golden brown.

- Add the chopped tomatoes, season with salt and turmeric, and cook until the tomatoes become slightly mushy.

- Sauté for a minute after adding the freshly prepared Malvani masala.Now add 1/2 cup tamarind water to cook for 2 to 3 minutes in the masala and with the tomatoes.

- Simmer the flame before adding the coconut milk and bringing it to a boil. Slowly add the marinated fish pieces to the boiling curry, along with any extra marinated masala that remains in the bowl.

- In the Malvani Fish Curry, add a little water to adjust the consistency and salt to taste.

- Stir the Malvani Fish Curry lightly. Simmer the Malvani fish curry for at least 10 minutes, or until the fish is completely cooked through.

- Turn off the heat when the Malvani Fish Curry is done. Check the salt and spices and adjust as needed. Serve the Malvani Fish Curry immediately in a serving bowl.

- To make a delicious lunch or dinner, serve the Malvani Fish Curry Recipe with some steamed rice, fish fry, and pickled onions on the side. It's also a great weekend lunch or dinner option.

# Malvani Mutton Sukka

34

Mutton Sukha Malvani - by the time I browsed this recipe from my mother cookbook, I was sure this would be a winning recipe. The spice that blends in this dish gives it a delicious flavor and you can serve it with Rice or Jowar Bhakri , Thecha (a very spicy paste of garlic and dried red peppers) and a raw onion. To balance the spice she use to serve this dish with Sol kadi.

Malvan being a coastal area of  Konkan,  have their own way of cooking food. Malvani cuisine uses loose coconut in various forms such as grated, dry grated, deep fried, coconut paste, and coconut milk. Many masalas contain dried red chillies and other spices such as coriander seeds, peppercorns, cumin, cardamom, ginger, garlic, etc.

**Preparation time:** 30 minutes
**Cooking time:** 45 minutes
**Serves:** 4

**Ingredients:**

- 500 gms Mutton

- 1/2 tsp Turmeric powder

- 1/4 tsp Asafoetida

- 2 tsp Ginger garlic paste

- 1 cup chopped Onion

- 5 tsp Masala Malvani

- 2 tsp Garam masala powder

- 2 - 3 tbsp Coconut Grated

- 3 - 4 Bay leaf1 stick piece Cinnamon

**Steps to prepare:**

- First you need to dry roast the coconut till its light brown in color. Make sure you do not burn it. Let it cool.

- Add the dry roasted coconut in the mixer. Add little water and grind it to a smooth paste. Set it aside.

- In a large bowl, add mutton, turmeric powder, salt, asafoetida, ginger garlic paste. Mix it well. Set it aside for 1 hour.

- Heat oil in a pan.

- Add bay leaf and cinnamon. Saute it well.

- Add onions and fry it till it turns translucent.

- Now add marinated chicken and mix it well. Add 1/2 cup of water.

- Cover it with lid and let it cook on a low flame till the mutton is cooked atleast 3/4.

- Add the ground coconut masala paste and Malvani masala.

- Cook till the mutton gets tenderly soft.

- Add garam masala and mix it well.

- Cook for another 10-15 minutes and turn off the heat.

- Serve it with hot chapatti or bhakri.

# Malvani Mutton Curry Muttonache Rassa

Muttonache Rassa is a traditional Malvani Mutton Curry from Maharashtra's South Konkan region and Goa. Malvani Mutton Curry is also known as Muttonache Rassa. It's a traditional Indian recipe from Maharashtra. The best spice mix for making traditional Maharashtrian spice powder requires a proper balance of whole spices. The aroma released when the spice mixture is ground to perfection. Mutton curry is a popular Maharashtrian dish, but it is simply spectacular when prepared in the Malvani style.

Mutton curry is a popular Maharashtrian dish of western India regional cuisine, especially when prepared in the Malvani style. Malvani style mutton curry is a simple mutton curry dish, but it's the way it's cooked that makes it so flavorful.

**Preparation time:**20 minutes
**Cooking time:**50 minutes
**Serves:**3

## Ingredients:

- 750-800 grams mutton on the bone

- 4 medium sized onions finely sliced

- 1-1/2 tablespoons ginger paste

- 1-1/2 tablespoons garlic paste

- 1/2 teaspoon turmeric powder

- Chopped coriander to garnish

- Oil

- Salt to taste

**For the masala:**

- 8 dried red chillies

- 6-8 peppercorns

- 1 tablespoon coriander seeds

- 3/4 teaspoon cumin seeds

- 3/4 teaspoon carraway seeds (shah jeera)

- 4 green cardamoms

- 2 black cardamoms

- 4-5 cloves

- 3/4 cup copra (dried coconut, grated)

- 1-1/2 teaspoons of khus khus, poppy seeds (substitute with 3-4 whole cashew nuts)

**Steps to prepare:**

- Wash and drain the mutton in a colander after cutting it into medium-sized pieces.

- You can either cook the mutton over a low heat in a kadai/pan (which will take at least 45 minutes –

1 hour for the mutton to become tender) or pressure cook it to expedite the process. Choose your cooking method wisely. See the notes for instructions on how to pressure cook the meat.

- In a heavy-bottomed kadai/pan, heat the oil and fry the sliced onions until golden. Then add the ginger and garlic paste and fry for a few seconds more.

- Fry the mutton pieces for a minute. Add 4 cups of water (total of 1 litre) and season with salt to taste. Cook over medium heat, covered, until the meat is tender. Depending on the quality of the meat, it could take 40-50 minutes or slightly longer.

- While the meat is cooking, dry roast all of the ingredients listed under 'For the masala' one at a time on a tawa/griddle and set aside to cool. Grind the spices (except for the roasted copra) to a fine powder. Then add the copra and about 1/2 to 3/4 cup of water (a little at a time) to make a fine paste. Keep the water from the mixer grinder aside.

- When the meat is tender, stir in the turmeric powder, ground masala, and reserved water. Adjust the salt to taste and continue to cook for another 8-10 minutes.

- Remove from the heat, top with chopped coriander, and serve with rice woday (wada), rice, or chapathis.

**Notes:**

- If you want to reduce the spice level, remove the seeds in the chillies but do not reduce the quantity.

- Transfer the cleaned meat to a pressure cooker, add salt and a little water, cover the lid, place the weight (whistle), and cook on high heat until the first whistle sounds. Cook for another 8-10 minutes on low heat. Turn off the heat and allow the cooker to cool to room temperature. Then open and inspect. Continue to cook for another 3-4 minutes if the meat is not done. The cooking time will vary depending on how tender the meat is.

# Surmai Fry (Malvani style)

43

Malvan is the  coastal region in the southern western state of Maharashtra, India, and is one of the most amazing destinations if you are looking to eat seafood. Traditionally fried for a crispy crust, Tawa Malvani fish is a delicacy that can be enjoyed all over Maharashtra. With Malvani Masala giving fish a brilliant flavor coated with rice flour making it crisp on the outside and soft and tender on the inside, is a sure to try fried fish recipe with cold drinks or sol kadi like the locals do!

**Preparation time:** 20 minutes
**Cooking time:** 15 minutes
**Serves:** 2

## Ingredients:

- 2 Big Size Surmai (Kingfish)

- 3 tsp Ginger Coriander Paste

- 1 tsp Ginger Garlic Paste

- Kokum/Lemon Juice - As required

- 3 tsp Malvani Masala

- 1/4 tsp Turmeric

- Salt as per taste

- Oil - For shallow frying

## For Coating:

- 3 tbsp Rice Flour

- 1 tbsp Sooji or Rava (Semolina)

- 1 tbsp Malvani Masala

- Salt as per taste

## Steps to prepare:

- Marinate the surmai for 5 minutes with salt and Kokam or lemon juice.

- Add the coriander chilli paste, ginger garlic paste, and malwani masala and coat each piece of fish thoroughly. You can add a little more kokum extract.

- Marinate the fish for at least half an hour before frying it (the more you marinate the better).

- In a plate, combine rice flour, rava (semolina), malvani Masala, and salt. You can substitute plain rice flour for the semolina. It tastes just as good!!

- Coat the marinated pieces of surmai with the coating.

- In a skillet or frying pan, heat some oil and shallow fry the fish. (Be careful not to overheat the oil or the coating will burn.) Also, make sure the fish is fried on both sides over a low flame.

46

# Pamphlet (Pomfret) Fry Recipe

The Malvani cuisine of Maharashtra's coastal Konkan region is one of the most distinct regional Indian cuisines. Malvani rava fish fry is a delicious and crunchy dish made with kingfish, mackerel, or pomfret. Fish contains a lot of calcium and phosphorus, as well as other nutrients that are good for the brain and body.

The addition of Kokum and Malwani masala lends a Malwani flavour to the fish fry. The coating contains rice flour and rava. Fish fry is popular in Maharashtra because it is crispy on the outside and tender on the inside. Malvani cuisine is predominantly non-vegetarian, with fried fish being one of the most popular dishes. After marinating in masalas, surmai, or king fish, is shallow fried.

Rava fish fry malvani style is a crispy fried fish recipe with a soft interior filled with masala. It's a crunchy fried fish recipe, but there's a lot more to it than that!

This Malvani Style Rava Pomfret Fish Fry is the claim to fame of Indian coastal cuisine. Because of the magical spice that hits you with the first bite, the flavour beneath the crunchy rava layer is delicious!

**Preparation Time:**10 minutes

**Cooking Time:**12 minutes

**Serves:**2

**Ingredients:**

- 2 medium size Pomfrets

- 1/2 cup rice flour

- 1/2 cup rawa

- 2 tbsp coriander powder

- 2 tbsp red chilli powder

- 1 tbsp black pepper

- 5 tbsp oil

- 1 tbsp lemon juice

- 1 tbsp salt

**Steps to prepare:**

- First, thoroughly wash the Pomfret and cut some slits in it.

- Now, squeeze half a lemon over the fish and sprinkle with tumeric powder. Refrigerate this for about 15 minutes to allow the lemon to fully absorb. This is an important step because it reduces the fish's fishy odour.

- Let's get started on the marinade, rice flour, and rawa mixture. In a small plate, combine Rawa and Rice flour in equal parts and set aside. It will be used to coat the fish before shallow frying them.

- Marinate the fish in a mixture of red chilli powder, turmeric powder, malvani masala, lime juice, kokum, and salt. After that, set aside for 5 minutes.

- In a bowl, combine the red chilli powder, black pepper, coriander powder, and salt, then add enough water to make a thick paste.

- Salt the rice flour and semolina together. Then, dab both sides of the fish with the semolina mixture.

- Heat the oil in the pan and add the fish. Then fry until crisp on both sides. Serve immediately.

# Malvani Bombil (Bombay Duck) Fry

Bombil Fry is a shallow fry preparation of the fish that has become associated with Maharashtra's seafood cuisine- Bombil or Bombay Duck.

Don't go by its apppearance, this fish is in high demand in the sea food market. When shallow fried with a Semolina and Rice-Flour coating, it achieves a crisp exterior with a soft and buttery interior. The succulent Bombil Fry is a popular dish on any sea food restaurant's menu.

Bombil is also known as Bombay Duck because it is found in and around the waters of Bombay (Mumbai). For the benefit of those who live outside of Mumbai, let me state right away that the Bombay Duck is a fish, not a duck. It is without a doubt one of the most popular fish among Mumbai residents. During the monsoon season, when fishing in the west coast sea water is prohibited, Mumbai residents prefer to purchase dried versions of this lizard fish. If you happen to be in Mumbai during the summer, you will see Bombil suspended with a rope tied across poles to dry up.

If you live near areas where fish are being dried out, this activity may prove to be a torturous exercise for your smell senses. The fish has a high moisture content, and when dried, it loses all of its moisture and resembles a small stick. So, if you're familiar with Mumbai slang, you'll understand why a thin person is referred to as Sukka Bombil (dried Bombay Duck).

**Preparation time:**60 minutes
**Cooking time:**20 minutes
**Serves:**4-5

## Ingredients:

- 5 Large sized=700gms Fresh Bombay Duck-Bombil

- 1-tsp Turmeric Powder

- 1 Lemon Juice

- 3 Green Chilies

- 7-8 Cloves of Garlic

- 1-inch Ginger root

- Cooking Oil

- ¾ Cup=150 gms Semolina (Bombay Rava)

- ½ Cup=75 gms Rice flour (can be replaced with Wheat Flour or Sorghum Flour)

- 4-tbsp Malvani Masala (or 3 tbsp Kashmiri red Chili Powder + 1-tbsp Garam Masala Powder)

- Salt

## Steps to prepare:

- Let's take a look at how to clean Bombay Duck fish. Spread a piece of paper on the board to keep it clean. A chopping board and a sharp knife are required. Place a fish on a cutting board. Remove the tail, head, and fins. Remove these parts with a sharp knife. Check that the cleaning knife is sharp.

Cut diagonally below the head and pull out the offal. Now it's time to cut the fins.

- Let us now remove its shells. Scrape off the shells with a knife's blunt edge, running it along its body from tail to head. Cut along its stomach and open the fish. We'll run the knife through its stomach along this faint line. Remove and discard the offal from the inside. Continue to go deeper and deeper until the fish is completely open. You can cut along using the centre bone as a guide. Switch to the other side. You can go a little deeper if it still does not appear completely flat. Don't go too deep. We don't want to divide it into two parts. In a moment, we'll clean the fish with water.

- Most of us don't know how to clean fish at home and must rely on vendors. Sometimes the vendor is overloaded with customers, and other times he is simply not an expert at cutting fish. Similarly, all Bombay Ducks will be cleaned.

- We'll now use water to wash and clean the fish. Pat dry with a kitchen napkin after cleaning with water. Marinate in a mixture of turmeric powder, salt, and lemon juice. Turmeric Powder has antibacterial and antiseptic properties. Lemon juice and turmeric powder aid in the removal of fish odour. Apply this mixture to both sides of the fish. Set aside for 10 minutes.

- After marinating the Bombay Duck for 10 minutes, we will proceed to the next step. Bombay

Duck has a high moisture content that must be removed for proper handling. We'll use a cutting board. You can cover any large flat object with a piece of cloth. Arrange the marinated fish on top of the cloth. Cover the fish with a second piece of cloth. Place a second chopping board or flat surface object. Place a large object or load on this board. Allow the fish to rest for 30 minutes.

- Grind the chilies, ginger, and garlic together for the second marination. With 1-2 tsp water, grind into a thick and coarse paste. The coarse paste is complete. While grinding, I used 1 teaspoon of water.

- Set it aside. Let's go check on the fish. Take off the board and the cloth. We removed the excess moisture, and the fish has firmed up.

- Put green masala paste on a large plate. Use this masala on all of the fish. The fish is now ready. We'll refrigerate for 10 minutes before frying. Keep refrigerated (Do not keep in deep freezer). This helps to firm up the fish and make it easier to handle while frying.

- Now we'll make a dry batter to fry the fish in. Combine Semolina, Rice Flour, and Malvani Masala in a large mixing bowl. If you don't have this Masala, you can substitute 3 tablespoons Kashmiri red chilli powder and 1 tablespoon Garam Masala powder. Mix in the salt to taste.

- Because this is a Rava fry, we used more Semolina/Rava in the batter. You can omit the Rava entirely and make a batter of rice flour, Malvani masala, and salt instead. You can keep this dry batter in the refrigerator and use it as needed for fish fry.

- Put some batter on a plate and set aside the rest. Remove the fish from the refrigerator and coat it in the batter. Apply the coating with care. We've heated up a pan. Let's begin frying the fish right now.

- In a pan, heat 2-3 tablespoons cooking oil. Reduce heat as the oil heats up and place a batter-coated fish in the pan to fry on low-medium heat. It is crucial to thoroughly heat the oil and tawa before frying the fish on low-medium heat.

- If the oil temperature is too low, the fish will stick to the pan and its skin may come off while changing sides. Such fried fish does not appear to be good enough to eat.

- We cooked the bottom for 3 minutes. Now switch sides. The underside is well cooked and appears to be crisp fried. Distribute the oil evenly around the tawa. Cook for 3 minutes more on the other side.

- After 3 minutes, remove from pan. Fry the remaining fish in more oil.

- Malvan Special-Crispy Bombil Rava Fry is now available.

# Baby Shark Curry - Mori Mutton

Moryechi xacuti, also known as mori mutton, is a spicy and delicious Goan shark fish curry. Baby shark is marinated in green masala and cooked in an onion, spice, and coconut curry. This dish can be paired with rice, Indian bread such as roti or chapati, or slice bread.

**Preparation time:**15 minutes
**Cooking time:**45 minutes
**Serves:**4

**Ingredients:**

- 
    1/2 kg small shark/baby shark

- 2 cups coconut grated

- 8 peppercorns

- 3 cloves

- 1 inch cinnamon stick

- 6 Kashmiri dry red chilies

- 1 teaspoon turmeric powder

- 10 garlic cloves

- 1 1/2 teaspoon coriander seeds

- 2 medium sized onions finely chopped

- 5 tablespoon Oil or as needed

- 1 marble sized ball tamarind

- 1 teaspoon turmeric powder

**For Marination:**

- 1 small bunch cilantro/coriander leaves

- 1 inch ginger

- 15 garlic pods

- 1 tablespoon turmeric powder

- 2 tablespoon red chili powder

**Steps to prepare:**

- Clean the baby shark and completely remove its skin. Cut into 1 to 2 inch pieces.

- The shark was cleaned, de-skinned, and chopped at the supermarket's fish counter.

- After washing the shark pieces, sprinkle them with turmeric powder, red chilli powder, and salt.

- Blend in the coriander leaves, ginger and garlic pods, and 1/2 cup water to make a paste. (Refer to the ingredients list in the marination section.)

- Apply the chopped baby shark pieces with this green masala paste. Place it in the freezer for 30 minutes to 1 hour.

- Now let's make gravy

- First chop the onions into small pieces and set it aside.

- In oil roast the spices (garam masala) such as black peppercorns, cloves, coriander seeds, cinnamon stick, and red chilies in a pan/kadai/wok for 2 minutes.

- After the spices have been roasted, add 3/4 of the chopped onions and fry until pinkish.

- Add the chopped garlic and cook until the raw garlic smell goes away.

- Then add the grated coconut and roast it on a low flame until it turns brownish.

- Stir in the tamarind and turn off the heat immediately.

- After turning off the heat, add turmeric powder. Mix it well.

- Add 1 cup water or as needed after cooling to make a medium consistent gravy. Set it aside.

- Fry the remaining chopped onions in a wok or kadai with 3 tablespoon oil. Fry for 10 minutes after adding the green masala marinated baby shark pieces.

- Pour the ground gravy into the onion shark mixture and cook for 30 minutes over low heat.

Stir frequently to prevent it from sticking to the bottom of the kadai.

- Add salt to taste after 30 minutes, or when the shark pieces are cooked, and garnish with chopped cilantro leaves.

# Chicken Malvani

Today, I am just not only going to share the recipe but also take you back to my childhood days when my mother use to cook this lip smacking and mouth watering Malvani recipe. A perfect start to Sunday is the smell of the alluring malvani masala when she use to mix it in chicken. My taste buds couldn't just resist the temptation till my mother use to give me a sample of gravy and chicken piece to taste. My hunger knew no boundaries after tasting it and I use to roam around kitchen only to hear her saying, "Wait I have to yet make kombdi vada." They say "Patience is bitter, but its fruit is sweet." No counts on how much vada orchicken I ate, it always use to be tickling my taste buds for more and off-course served with motherly love. What else you need!

This recipe can be enjoyed only when we eat it hot and to make it complete, serve it with Sol kadi and tomato onion salad. Mouth watering isn't it?

**Preparation time:**10 minutes
**Cooking time:**1 hour 10 minutes
**Serves:**6

Let's start with Malvani Chicken curry:

**Ingredients:**
**We need to first marinate chicken:**

- 1 kg. Chicken, cut and washed

- 1 tbsp. Ginger Garlic paste

- Salt as per taste

- 1 tbsp lemon juice

- 1/4 cup Coriander leaves

- 1/2 tsp Red chilli powder

- 1/4 Turmeric powder

*For Malvani masala: You can get the malvani masala from the local market, but my mother made this at home.*

- 6-7 dry red chillies (Bedgi Mirchi recommended)

- 1/4 cumin seeds

- 1/4 tsp Mustard seeds

- 1/2 tsp Aniseed (saunf)

- 1 inch Cinnamon, Dalchini

- 1/2 tsp Aniseed, chakra phool

- 4 cloves, laung

- 10 black pepper

- 1 black cardamom, Badi elaichi

- 1 tsp Sesame seeds, til

- 1 tsp poppy seeds, khus khus

- 1 blade mace, javitri

- 1/4 tsp fenugreek seeds

**For Onion coconut paste:**

- 1 sliced Onion

- 1 cup grated coconut (I used dry coconut powder)

**For cooking chicken:**

- 1 Bay leaf

- 3 chopped Onions

- 1 tsp Ginger Garlic paste

- 1 tsp Red Chilli powder

- 1/4 tsp Turmeric powder

- 2 tsp Corinder powder

- 4 tbsp Cooking oil

**Steps to prepare:**
**Let's marinate the chicken first:**

- In a mixing bowl, add chicken, ginger garlic paste, salt, lemon juice, coriander leaves, red chilli powder and turmeric powder.

- Mix it well and keep is it aside for 30 minutes to 1 hour.

**Now, let's make Malvani masala:**

- Heat pan and dry roast red chillies till they become crisp.

- Set it aside in a plate.In the same pan heat oil and add the remaining spices mentioned.

- Roast it till it releases an aromatic smell.

- Now, grind all the ingredients in mixer. Do not add water.

**Next, Onion Coconut paste:**

- In a pan add 1 tsp. of Oil and onion slices. Saute then for few seconds.

- Add grated coconut and saute till the coconut turns golden brown in color. Let it cool down.

- Then grind it to a fine paste.

**Making curry:**

- In a deep bottom vessel heat oil.

- Add bay leaf and saute for few seconds.

- Add onions and saute till translucent.

- Add ginger garlic paste and cook till the raw smell leaves.

- Add red chilli powder, turmeric powder and coriander powder.

- Saute it.Add marinated chicken pieces and mix it well.

- Add malvani masala powder and mix it well.

- Cover it and let it cook for about 5-10 minutes.

- Keep stirring in between.

- When the oil starts to separate from the chicken and the spices add coconut onion paste. Mix it well and let it cook for about 2 minutes.

- Add water as per consistency and add salt. Mix it well and cook for 10-20 minutes or till the chicken gets tender.

- The Malvani chicken is ready.

# Tessrya Masala Malvani

A mouthwatering clams gravy and a personal favourite made in almost every coastal household. This flavorful coconut-based gravy is sure to please. It goes well with steamed rice, chapati, or bhakri.

**Preparation time:**30 minutes
**Cooking time:**30 minutes
**Serves:**8

**Ingredients:**

- 3 kg Tisre (Clams)

- 1 medium fresh coconut split in two halves

- 2 medium onions whole

- 1 large potato cubed (Optional)

- 1/2 inch ginger, sliced

- A small whole head of garlic

- 3 tsp fennel seeds

- 2 tsp coriander seeds

- 3 cloves

- 4-5 peppercorns

- 2 petals of star anise

- 1 cm cinnamon stick

- 1 tsp turmeric powder

- 2 tbsp malvani masala

- 4-5 kokam

- alt to taste (If required, clams release their salty juices while cooking so add salt only after tasting)

- 2 tbsp Oil

## Steps to prepare:

- Prepare the clams by thoroughly washing them under running water 2-3 times. Put the clams in a large container. Place it on a medium flame and cover with a lid. Add no water at all. After 3 minutes, remove the lid partially.

- After another 2 minutes, check the clams. They must be open right now. Toss the clams so that the clams at the bottom rise to the surface. If all of the clams are open, turn off the heat. Allow to cool completely.

- To make the gravy, char roast 2 onions, the garlic head, and the coconut halves over a gas burner. With1 tsp oil roast the spices and ginger in a small pan.

- Grate the coconut which is roasted. Remove the outer layer from the onions and garlic. Use no more than 7-8 garlic cloves. The remainder can be used for any other purpose. Chop the onion into large chunks.

- Finely grind the coconut, onions, garlic, ginger, spices, turmeric, and malvani masala.

- The clams will be completely cool by this point. Separate the empty clam shells to sort the clams. Take the clam shells that contain the meat. Remove the empty ones. Consider removing the closed. Do not discard the liquid in the vessel.

- After sorting the clams, strain the liquid through a muslin cloth to remove any small sand grains from the clams.

- Heat the oil in a large kadai, making it easy to stir the clams. If you are using potatoes, add them now. Mix in the ground paste. Stir for about 2 minutes.

- To this, add the clam strained clam juices. Cook it covered, until the potatoes are tender.

- If you are not using potatoes, add the clams after you have added the clam juices. Mix in the kokum. Cook for about 5-7 minutes. Turn off the heat and serve immediately with chapati or rice. The next day, these taste even better.

# Bangda Tikhla (Mackerel fish curry)

Malvani cuisine includes a wide variety of vegetarian and non-vegetarian dishes, but it is best known for its seafood preparations and creative use of spices. Malvani cuisine, which originated in the Southern Konkan belt, incorporates elements of Maharashtrian and Goan cuisines into its regional cuisine. Coconut is used in a variety of ways, including fresh, grated, coconut milk, and paste. In addition to coconut, rice, and a variety of spices such as cumin seeds, red chilies, tirphal (a type of schezwan unique to the Konkan belt), and souring agents such as kokum, tamarind, and raw mango are used in the preparation of the food.

This dish is made with mackerel fish. Tikhla refers to a hot and sour thicker curry made with coconut milk. Bangda tikhla is traditionally served with fresh chapatti or bhakri.

**Preparation time:**10 minutes
**Cooking time:**30 minutes
**Serves:**2-3

## Ingredients:

- 5 nos Bangda (Indian Mackerel)

- 100 gms Coconut, grated

- 7 nos Red Chillies (Bedgi Mirchi)

- ¼ tsp Haldi (Turmeric) Powder

- 1 small Onion, chopped

- 4 nos Tirphal (type of Schezwan Pepper/Zanthoxylum rhetsa)

- 6 nos Kokum

- 3 nos Black Pepper

- ¾ tsp Coriander Seeds

- Water as required

## Steps to prepare:

- To make a thick paste, grind coconut, red chilies, coriander seeds, black peppercorns, haldi powder, 1/2 portion onion, tirphal, and water as needed.

- In a pan, heat the oil. Sauté for a few minutes with the remaining chopped onion and paste.

- Now add kokum, bangda (Indian Mackerel), salt, and water as needed. Cook for 7–8 minutes, covered.

- Garnish with coriander leaves if desired. Serve immediately.

# Prawns Tawa Masala (Kolambi Tawa Masala)

Prawns Tawa Masala, also known as Kolambi Tawa Masala, is a popular spicy and tangy dish. Malvani masala is a blend of 15 to 16 dry spices and powder masala. Kolambi Masala is a Marathi prawn stew prepared in a spicy coconut gravy. This dish is commonly consumed on India's western coast. Prawns are cooked in a spicy coconut stew with curry leaves, cumin, and chilies. This is a Marathi recipe for Kolambi Masala. Kolambi is available on the menus of all Maharastrian restaurants.

Malvani cuisine can be traced back to Malvan, a majestic town in the Sindhudurg district on Maharashtra's west coast. The Malvan coast offers a dizzying array of cuisines based on fish, fowl, and vegetables, but seafood and chicken recipes take centre stage in any Malvani meal.

Malvan, a coastal town in Konkan, has its own distinct style of cooking.

Image Credit: From my Kitchen1

**Preparation time:**15 minutes
**Cooking time:**25 minutes
**Serves:**4

**Ingredients:**

- Coriander Leaves

- 2 Tbsp Oil

- 1 Tbsp Garlic (Crushed)

- 1/2 Tsp Cumin Seeds

- 1/2 Tsp Asafoetida

- 1 Sprig Curry Leaves

- 2 Tsp Green Chillies (Crushed)

- 250 Gms Prawns (Marinated With Salt +Turmeric)

- 1 Tsp Red Chilli Powder

- 1/2 Tsp Garam masala Powder

- 1 Tbsp. Oil

- 3 Green Chillies

- Coriander Leaves

**Steps to prepare:**

- On a tawa, heat the oil and add the crushed garlic, cumin seeds, asafetida, curry leaves, and crushed green chilies. Mix thoroughly.

- Mix in the marinated prawns.

- After that, add some garam masala and red chilli powder.

- Cook on high heat, stirring constantly. Add a little more oil if necessary.

- Spread the prawns evenly across the tawa to ensure even cooking.

- Don't keep stirring because it will break up.

- Turn them after about 3 minutes.

- The prawns will be perfectly cooked after about 3 minutes.

- If you are not truly happy, cook them for another 4-5 minutes, turning them halfway through.

- Turn off the heat and add the green chilies and coriander leaves.

- The prawn tawa masala is now ready for serving.

# Kolambi Bhaat Malvani Style (Prawns Rice)

This Indian Prawn Rice recipe comes from Malvan in Maharashtra's Sindhudurg District, the state's southernmost district. Kolambi Bhaat is made with rice, prawns, and whole spices.

This traditional Maharashtrian dish has a long history. In this popular Indian dish, spices are combined with prawns before rice is added. This aromatic, spicy, and flavorful kolambi bhaat recipe is seasoned with fresh handcrafted Malvani masala. This delicious prawn rice with raita is a quick, easy, and delicious weeknight supper.

**Preparation time:**20 minutes
**Cooking time:**30 minutes
**Serves:**3-4

**Ingredients:**

**For Green Masala**

- 1 cup roughly chopped Coriander leaves

- 6 Garlic cloves

- 1" Ginger, roughly chopped

- 4 Green chillies, roughly chopped

- 2 tbsp grated Coconut

## For Rice

- 6 cups Water

- Salt

- 1½ cup Basmati rice, soaked for 45 min

## For Prawns marination

- 1/2 kg Prawn, 50 count to a kg prawns

- Salt to taste

- 1 tbsp juice of Lime

- 1/2 tsp Turmeric powder

- 1/4 tsp Coriander powder

- 1/4 tsp Red chilli powder

## For Masala

- 3 tbsp Clarified butter

- 3 Green Cardamom

- 2" Cinnamon stick

- 1 Bay leaf

- 1 large Onion, sliced

- Green masala

- 1½ tsp Malvani masala

- Salt to taste

- 1/4 cup water

- 1½ tbsp Yoghurt, whipped

- 2 tbsp Coriander leaves, chopped

- Coriander sprigs for garnish

## Steps to prepare:

- First lets make green masala: With 3 tbsp water, blend all the ingredients mentioned in green masala to a smooth paste and set aside.

- Lets cook rice. Bring water and salt to a boil. Cook the rice until it is 95% done.Transfer out and reserve.

- Next, marinate the prawns. Marinate the prawns with salt, lime juice, and turmeric powder. After that, set aside for 10 minutes.

- Now lets prepare masala. Sauté the cardamom, cinnamon, and bay leaf in clarified butter until fragrant. Add the onions and cook until they turn golden brown.

- Mix in the green masala, koli masala, and salt.

- Then cook for 2–3 minutes. Mix in a little water with the yoghurt.

- Mix in the prawns thoroughly.

- Then cook for 2–3 minutes.

- Simmer for 5 minutes, covered.

- Mix in the coriander leaves and lemon juice.

- Combine the prawn masala and the cooked rice. Serve immediately.

# Veg Recipes

# Padwal Bhaji Malvani (Snake Gourd)

Padwal bhaji is a simple yet tasty dish made with snake gourd as the main ingredient. You can also try this fantastic bhaji in other combinations. Padwal bhaji with chana dal is a popular Malvan dish.

Padwal bhaji is also an excellent complement to a low-calorie keto diet plan. The following are some of the health benefits of this bhaji:

1. It is extremely effective for weight loss.

2. It improves your breathing.

3. Clear the kidneys of impurities.

4. It is an anti-anxiety tonic.

5. It benefits your skin's health.

6. It is high in vitamin B3, which is necessary for good health.

7. It helps to improve your digestive system.

If you want to reap these health benefits and try this delicious Malvani recipe. Follow the detailed Maharashtrian recipe provided below and enjoy this superb bhaji. Served in all Maharashtra Indian food restaurants.

**Preparation time:** 15 minutes
**Cookiing time:** 15 minutes
**Serves:** 3

## Ingredients:

- 250 gms Padwal (Snake Gourd) finely cut

- 1 pc Onion, finely chopped

- 1 pc, Tomato, finely chopped

- 6-7 cloves Garlic, chopped

- 3 tbsp Coconut oil

- 1/3 tsp Cumin seeds

- 1/3 tsp Mustard seeds

- 1/3 tsp Turmeric powder

- 1 tsp Red chili powder

- Salt

- 1/4 cup Water

**Coconut masala:**

- 3-4 Green chilies

- 1/2 cup Coconut, chopped

- Water as per requirement

**Steps to prepare:**

- In a blender, combine green chilies, chopped coconut, and a little water.Blend until the ingredients form a fine paste. Set aside the masala.

- In a pan, heat the oil. Allow the mustard seeds to crackle. Stir in the finely chopped garlic and cumin seeds for a few seconds. Cook for a few seconds, or until the garlic begins to brown.

- Add onions and let it cook for 2-3 minutes, until the onion turns light brown, on a medium flame.

- Mix in the turmeric and chilli powder. Cook for about 30 seconds on low heat.

- Now add tomatoes. Cover the pan and cook for 4-5 minutes on low heat until the tomatoes are soft.

- Stir in the Padwal for a few seconds, then add the salt and mix well.

- Pour in the water, cover the pan, and cook for 15-17 minutes, or until it is thoroughly cooked and tender.

- Combine the prepared coconut masala. Cook for 1 minute after thoroughly mixing.

- Padwal Bhaji is finished and ready to serve with hot rice or chapatti.

## Remember:

- When cutting the Padwal, make sure to remove the pith and seeds because they don't taste good.

- Tomato paste should never be used. Instead, use chopped tomatoes to improve the flavour of the recipe.

# Kala Vatana Amti

Black Vatana or Black Peas Curry is one of Malvani food's many Indian vegetarian dishes. Maharashtrian and Goan cuisines have influenced it. The Malvani people make extensive use of both wet and dry spices in their traditional Indian dishes. Malvani cuisine is dominated by fish dishes.

**Preparation time:**15 minutes
**Cooking time:**35 minutes
**Serves:**3

**Ingredients:**

- 1½ cup Kala vatana / Bengal gram

- 1 tbsp Oil

- 1 small Onion, sliced

- 1 tbsp Ginger, chopped

- 6 cloves Garlic, crushed, chopped

- 1/2 cup Coconut, grated

- 1 tsp Red chilli powder

- 1 tsp Turmeric powder

- 1 tsp Coriander powder

- 1½ tsp Malvani masala

- 1/4 cup Water

- 2 tbsp Oil

- 1 small Onion, chopped

- 1 Tomato, chopped

- Salt - as per taste

- 1 tbsp Coriander leaves

**Steps to prepare:**

- One night before, soak the kala vatana. Drain and set aside for the next morning.

- Cook the black peas in a pressure cooker with a few cups of water for about 10 minutes. Allow to cool before setting aside.

- Heat up the oil and add onions. Then cook until the onions are light brown.

- Mix in the ginger and garlic.

- Add and sauté the coconut in the pan.

- Combine the red chilli powder, turmeric powder, coriander powder, and malvani masala in a mixing bowl. Then thoroughly combine.

- Remove from the heat and set aside to cool.

- Then pour in 1/4 cup of water.

- Finally, using a food processor, make a smooth paste and set aside.

- In the same pan, heat the oil and sauté the onions until they are light brown. Add the tomatoes and cook until they are soft. Add the masala paste and salt to taste. Then bring it to a boil. Cook for 10 minutes after adding the boiled kala vatana. Mix in the coriander leaves.

# Mulyachi Bhaji (Raddish veg)

In coastal Malvani cuisine, Mooli ki Sabzi is known as Mulyachi Bhaji.

Mulyachi bhaji is a popular Malvan dish made with only a few ingredients. It has that delicious taste for which Malvani bhajis are famous. All you need is radish and its leaves to enjoy the delightful taste of Mulyachi bhaji.

Mulyachi Bhaji is a popular and simple dry dish. Mulyachi is a northern Indian word for radish, also known as Mooli. Chana dal is used in this recipe. Mulyachi / radish / moli bhaji or sabzi is a highly aromatic dish. Its strong flavour can be tempered by using tomato puree. Fresh coriander leaves add a unique flavour to this recipe. This dish, which is served for lunch or dinner, is very popular in Maharashtra and Goa.

**Preparation time:**10 minutes
**Cooking time:**30 minutes
**Serves:**4

**Ingredients:**

- 1 cup Radish, grated

- 1 cup Radish leaves, finely chopped

- 2 tbsp Oil

- A pinch of Asafoetida

- 1/2 tsp Mustard seeds

- 1/2 tsp Cumin seeds

- 3-4 Green chilies, finely chopped

- 1 Onion, chopped

- 1 cup Coriander leaves, chopped

- 1/2 inch of Ginger, grated

- 1/2 tsp Turmeric powder

- 1 tsp Cumin powder

- Salt

- 2 tsbp Coconut, grated

- 1/2 cup cooked Bengal gram

**Steps to prepare:**

- In a pot, heat the oil. Stir in the asafoetida and mustard seeds. When they begin to crackle, add the cumin seeds and green chilies and cook for a few seconds.

- Add the onion, chopped. For about 1 minute, move the spoon slightly.

- Make a paste of coriander leaves and ginger and add it to the dish.

- Stir in the turmeric powder, cumin powder, and salt for about one minute.

- Stir in the sliced radish and radish leaves for about a minute. Allow it to cook in its own water, which the radish will shed after a while, covered with a lid, until the radish is soft and tender. Check the vegetable frequently while cooking to see if it is done.

- Stir in the grated coconut and cook for about 2 minutes.

- Mulayachi Bhaji is ready to serve with rice, Chapatti, or Nan.

- **(Optional)** -Add 1/2 cup cooked Bengal gramme or Chana dal between steps 2 and 3. Mix it thoroughly.

# Kaju Curry Olya Kaju chi Bhaji

The Malvan region is well-known for its Kaju Curry. Because of the abundance of cashews in the region, cashew curry is a well-known and traditional Malvani dish. Olya kajuchi bhaji (cashew nut bhaji) is a popular Konkani dish in the Malvani region, where the tender cashews are cooked in a spicy curry. Cashews are widely used in Indian cuisine, and this ingredient is a must-have for any Indian restaurant because it is used in a variety of dishes.

Curry with wet fresh cashew nuts. Fresh/delicate cashew nuts arrive in India during the summer, primarily in March. Tandalachi bhakri (Rice Bhakri) complements malvani kaju masala or kajuchi rassa bhaji. Oly kajuchi bhaji is a traditional Konkani dish from Maharashtra.

**Preparation time:**30 minutes
**Cooking time:** 30 minutes

**Ingredients:**
**For Coconut paste:**

- 4 Garlic cloves

- 1" Ginger, chopped

- 1/2 cup grated Coconut

- 3 Green chillies

**For Bhaji**

- 2 tbsp Oil

- Pinch of asafoetida

- 1/2 tsp Mustard seeds

- 2 medium Onions, chopped

- 10 Curry leaves

- 1 Tomato, finely chopped

- 1/2 tsp Turmeric powder

- 1 tsp Malvani masala

- Salt to taste

- 2 cups of tender Cashew nuts, soaked in hot water for 2 hours

- 1 small Potato, boiled } cut into 1/2 inch cubes

- 1½ cup Water

- 1½ tbsp chopped Coriander leaves

## Steps to prepare

- Reserve the coconut mixture after blending the ingredients to a smooth paste.

- In a pan, heat the oil and add the asafoetida and mustard seeds. Allow it to crackle.

- Combine the onions and curry leaves in a mixing bowl. Then fry until the onions are translucent.

- Next, add tomatoes and fry until the tomatoes are soft and the oil separates from the masala.

- Then add the turmeric powder, malvani masala, and salt. Then thoroughly combine.

- Mix in the soaked cashews and boiled potatoes. Then thoroughly combine.

- Simmer for 5 minutes, covered.

- Add water and bring it to a boil. Simmer for 10 minutes, covered.

- Cook over medium heat until the gravy reaches the desired consistency.

- Mix in the coriander leaves. Then serve immediately with bhakris and chapatis.

# Gavar Bhopla Chi Bhaji

Gavar Phali is the vernacular name for Cluster Beans. Gavar Bhopla Chi Bhaji is a sweet cum spicy Malvan dish that you can cook by using pumpkin pieces and green cluster bean pods as the main ingredients and the Goda masala as the essential part. Only a few ingredients and the simple preparation may be why it is a traditional dish on funeral occasions in Maharashtrian cuisine and culture. You will find this on the menu in many local Indian restaurants in the region.

Here are some of the health benefits that this fantastic dish can provide:

1. Ideal for losing weight.

2. It strengthens the bones.

3. It is a blessing for those suffering from diabetes.

4. Excellent for heart health.

5. Unrivaled in terms of blood circulation regulation.

So, if you want to improve your health and add some variety to your daily cooking, Gavar Bhopla Chi Bhaji is a must-try.

**Preparation time:** 15 minutes
**Cooking time:** 20 minutes
**Serves:** 4

## Ingredients:

- 1 cup Cluster beans, chopped

- 1 cup Pumpkin , coarsely chopped

- 2 tsp Red chili powder

- 1/2 tsp Turmeric powder

- A pinch of Hing (asafoetida)

- 4-5 Green chilies, chopped

- 1 tsp Cumin seeds

- 1 tsp Mustard seeds

- 1 tsp Fenugreek seeds

- 1 tsp Chili garlic paste

- Salt, as per your taste

- 1 inch Jaggery

- 2 tbsp Coconut, grated

- 1 cup Coriander leaves, finely chopped

- 1 tsp Coriander powder

- 4-5 Green curry leaves

- 4 tbsp Oil

- Water

- 1 tsp Goda Masala

**Steps to cook:**

- Heat four tablespoons of oil in a pot for a few minutes, then add the mustard seeds and let them crackle. Stir in the cumin seeds, fenugreek seeds, asafoetida, turmeric powder, curry leaves, and coriander leaves for about a minute.

- Stir in the par-boiled cluster beans for 2 minutes on medium heat.

- Stir in the pumpkin pieces for about 2 minutes on high heat.

- Add water and cover the pot with lid.

- Cook for a few minutes (about 10-12 minutes) on low heat until the pumpkin is soft.

- Mix in the coriander powder, red chilli powder, jaggery, and salt.

- Cook for about 1 minute on low heat with the pot covered.

- Turn off the heat and then stir in the coconut paste.

- Finish with a garnish of chopped coriander leaves.

# Vatpachi dal

Vatpachi dal is a traditional Malvan dish. In winter, having hot soup, dal, or saar is next level satisfaction. It appears simple, but it tastes fantastic. This is my absolute favourite dal. It has a nice texture and consistency. This is a simple but nutritious recipe. It can be made with ingredients that you already have in your pantry. It doesn't require a lot of ingredients. It is also referred to as godi dal. We have already seen a lot of dal recipes, such as Maharashtrian amti, fodniche varan, dalitoy, masoor amti, katachi amti, Solapuri amti, and so on. Another delightful and healthy addition to the list. You can make this at home.

This vatpachi godi dal is very simple to make. It tastes fantastic. Malvan is well-known for its cuisine. This is a comfort food that can also be served as soup. This dal can be prepared in a variety of ways. But today I'm going to show you my personal favourite. So, what are we waiting for? Let's get started.

Image Credit: Madhura's Recipe2

**Preparation time:** 10 minutes
**Cooking time:** 30 minutes
**Serves:** 3

**Ingredients:**

- 1/2 cup Tur dal

- 1 1/2 cup Water

- 1 medium size finely chopped Tomato

- 1/4 cup grated fresh Coconut

- 5~6 Garlic cloves

- 2~3 Green chilies

- 1/2 tsp Cumin seeds

- 2 tsp Oil

- 1/2 tsp Mustard seeds

- 1/2 tsp Cumin seeds

- A pinch of Hing

- Curry leaves

- 1/4 tsp Turmeric powder

- Water to adjust the consistency

- Salt to taste

**Steps to prepare:**

- Wash the tur dal thoroughly. 2-3 times with water and tomato, tomato, tomato

- Cook the dal in a pressure cooker on medium heat for 3 whistles.

- To make vatan or vatap, combine fresh coconut, garlic, green chilies, and cumin seeds in a blender jar and blend until smooth.

- If necessary, add a splash of water. The dal vatan or vatap is ready.

- Mix the cooked dal thoroughly.In a pan, heat the oil over medium heat and add the mustard seeds.

- When the mustard seeds begin to pop, add the cumin seeds, hing, curry leaves, and blended masala.

- Cook everything together for 3-4 minutes.

- Mix in the turmeric powder thoroughly.

- Mix in the cooked dal, water, and salt.

- Malvani dal is ready after about 7-8 minutes of simmering on medium heat.

- You can eat it plain as soup.It's also delicious with tandalachi bhakari or rice.

# Mirchiche Varan

Konkani Varan is a spicy lentil dish made without the use of oil.

Varan is a Maharashtrian Dal dish that is made with Dal. It is a one-of-a-kind delicacy that is served not only as part of a Maharashtrian family's daily meal but also as a wedding highlight. Typically served on the Thali menu of Maharashtra restaurants.

A plate of varan will almost certainly be included in a traditional Maharashtra thali. It's a simple family dish made of cooked rice and seasoned curry made with Toor dal (split pigeon peas). A dollop of sajuk tup over steaming hot varan bhaat with a lemon slice and some chutney or pickle on the side is a traditional Maharashtrian's definition of bliss. This dal dish is typical of Malvani cuisine.

Varan translates to "boiled lentil." A traditional Maharashtrian varan made from Toor dal is untempered. It's a simple lentil dish made with dal, turmeric, asafoetida, salt, and jaggery. This dal is also available in a tempered form known as phodaniche varan.

**Preparation time:**5 minutes
**Cooking time:**10 minutes
**Serves:**4

## Ingredients:

- 1 cup Masoor Dal, Red lentils split

- 2 Green Chillies, choppes

- 1 sprig Curry leaves

- 1 tbsp Coriander leaves, chopped

- 2 Kokum blades

- 1/2 cup Coconut, grated, blended

- Salt, to taste

- A pinch of Sugar

- 1/2 tsp Turmeric powder

- Asafoetida (1/8th teaspoon)

- Ghee (2 teaspoons)

- Mustard seeds

**Steps to prepare:**

- Boil one and a half cups of water. Cook the dal under pressure. Allow to cool and set aside.

- To make a paste of the cooked dal, add it to a deep-bottomed pan. Bring to a boil with the turmeric, coconut, kokum, salt, sugar, curry leaves, coriander leaves, and green chilies. Allow for a 5-minute simmer. Allow the flavours to infuse the dal for a minute after thoroughly mixing.

- In a tadka pan, heat the oil. Allow the asofoetida to crackle. Pour over the dal and sprinkle with mustard seeds.

# Vaalachi Rassa Bhaaji

Vaalachi Rassa Bhaaji is a delightful Maharashtrian-style curry made with vaal beans and potatoes and cooked with common masalas. For an everyday meal, serve Vaalachi Rassa Bhaaji with Steamed Rice and Lauki Raita. It goes well with Bhakri and Lehsuni Dal.

Vaalachi Rassa Bhaaji is a Maharashtrian dish that uses 'Kadve Vaal' and coconuts. In English, kadve vaal are known as 'field beans.' In India, we have various types of vaal, such as Kadve Vaal (bitter field beans), Goade Vaal (dalimbi / sweet field beans), Surati Vaal, Pavta, and so on.

Field beans are related to Broad beans and are smaller in size. They are high in protein, as well as vitamins A, B-Complex, C, and E, as well as minerals and enzymes!
Kadve Vaal is commonly used to make this curry vegetable or in the preparation of 'vaalache birde.' This gravy can also be made with Gode vaal / Dalimbi. Vaal is typically used in its dry form. They are soaked before sprouting and being used in vegetables.

Image Credit: Archana's Kitchen3

**Preparation time:**35 minutes
**Cooking time:**35 minutes

**Ingredients:**

- 11/2 cups sprouted and peeled Vaal Beans

- 1 Potato

- 1 finely chopped Onion

- 1/2 finely chopped Tomato

- 1/2 tsp Turmeric powder (Haldi)

- 1/2 tsp Red Chilli powder

- 1 tsp Kashmiri Red Chilli Powder

- 1 tsp Garam masala powder

**For Roasting:**

- 2 tsp Oil

- 1/2 thinly sliced Onion

- 3/4 cup grated Fresh coconut

- 2 cloves Garlic

- 1/4 inch Ginger

**For tempering**

- 2 tsp Oil

- 1/2 tsp Mustard seeds (Rai/ Kadugu)

- 1/4 tsp Asafoetida (hing)

- 1 sprig Curry leaves

## Steps to prepare:

- 
  To begin making the Vaalachi Rassa Bhaaji Recipe, we must begin two nights ahead of time. To begin, soak the dried vaal in plenty of water overnight.

- Drain all of the water and wash them again in clear water the next morning. Drain all of this water and keep it covered in a vessel until nightfall, or tie it up in a clean cotton or muslin cloth and keep it covered in a vessel until nightfall.

- Put the vessel somewhere warm. This will enable it to sprout well.

- Start by removing the sprouted vaal from the cloth and soak it in enough water overnight. This will make it easier to loosen the vaal peels the next morning.

- Peel all of the vaal the next morning and set aside.

- In a heavy-bottomed pan, heat the oil. When it's hot, add the sliced onions and cook until they're soft and translucent.

- Add and roast until the grated coconut is lightly browned. Now add the garlic and ginger and roast for a minute or two with the coconut.

- Remove from the heat and set aside to cool. Grind it with enough water to make a smooth paste.

- Set aside the finely chopped onion and tomato. Peel and cube the potatoes and keep them in clean water until ready to use.

- Meanwhile, heat a saucepan and add the oil for tempering. When the oil begins to heat, add the mustard seeds. When they begin to sputter, add the asafoetida and curry leaves and mix well.

- Sauté the chopped onions until they turn translucent. Sauté the turmeric powder and red chilli powder now. Cook for one minute.

- Mix in the cubed potatoes. Cook for 5-7 minutes, covered, with enough water to cover the potato cubes.

- Now, add the sprouted peeled vaal. To cook the potatoes and vaal, mix well and add more water as needed. Continue to stir occasionally.

- Add the chopped tomato and mix well when the potatoes are half cooked. Cook, stirring occasionally, covered.

- When the potatoes and vaal are tender, add the garam masala powder, ground coconut paste, and salt to taste.

- It is important to ensure that the vaal is not undercooked or overcooked.

- If necessary, add some water to make a medium-strength gravy. Bring to a boil, then reduce to a low heat for a few minutes.

- Check the seasoning, then remove from the heat and transfer to a serving bowl.

- For an everyday meal, serve Vaalachi Rassa Bhaaji Recipe with Steamed Rice and Lauki Raita. It goes well with Bhakri and Lehsuni Dal.

# Other Malvani Cuisines

# Sol Kadhi

Malvani food is traditionally served with a drink. Solkadhi is the name of that particular drink. It is a pink-colored drink, and the recipe for Sol Kadhi entices you to try it, and once you do, you will undoubtedly want to drink it again and again.

This drink's popularity stems not only from its lovely colour and creamy texture, but also from its numerous health benefits:

- It aids digestion by cooling the stomach.

- It is an effective treatment for acidity.

- It aids in weight loss.

- Its cooling effect also makes the skin appear healthy, rejuvenated, and lovely.

**Preparation time:**5 minutes
**Cooking time:**15 minutes

**Serves:**2

**Ingredients:**

- 6-8 Kokum or Aamsol

- 1 Cup Coconut, grated

- 1 Cup Hot water

- 2 cloves Garlic or 1 tsp of ginger

- 1-2 Green chillies

- A pinch of Asafoetida (heeng)

- To taste Rock salt

- For garnishing Coriander leaves

**Steps to prepare:**

- Soak the kokum in 3/4 cup water, along with the asafoetida and salt. Set aside for 3–4 hours.

- In a blender or mixer, combine the grated coconut, garlic, and chillies with a little water. When it reaches a thick paste-like consistency, squeeze the'milk' out of the paste and set aside.

- Add another 3/4 cup of water to the dry ingredients and mix for another minute or so. Extract the milk again, this time adding it to the original extract.

- Repeat this process two or three times more until all of the'milk' has been extracted from the coconut.

- **NOTE:**This process can be repeated several times, but keep in mind that the milk becomes thinner with each successive extraction.

- Remove the kokum from the water and combine it with the coconut milk mixture to make a creamy pink solkadhi.

- Adjust the seasoning to taste.

- Set aside for at least an hour.

- **NOTE:**Allow the Solkadhi to rest for at least an hour before consuming it.

- Serve chilled, garnished with fresh coriander leaves.

**Tip: Remember to stir the Kadhi every time you serve it because the coconut extract tends to rise to the top if the kadhi is left untouched for a while!**

# Amboli - Malvani Cuisine Breakfast

124

Malvani Amboli is a type of thick pancake made from rice and urad dal. Amboli is a traditional Malvani dish. It can be served as an evening snack or as an Indian breakfast recipe.

Amboli/ Tandalyachya Ambolya (Classic Maharashtrian Bread) is a traditional Maharashtrian bread recipe that is similar to Dosa but tastes slightly different. The batter's consistency, which must not be too thin or thick, is critical to obtaining the perfect-textured Amboli.

Amboli is a thick pancake made from rice and split black grams (urad dal). It is a thicker, fermented rice batter-based Dosa variation. The difference is in the dals or lentils used to make this batter. The next morning, thick Ambolis are made after the batter has fermented overnight.

**Prepration time:**15 minutes
**Cooking time:**30 minutes
**Soaking and Fermenting:**18 hours
**Serves:**6-7

**Ingredients:**

- 1 cup Rice

- 1/2 cup White lentils

- 1/2 tsp Fenugreek seeds

- Water for soaking

- Salt

- 1/4 cup Water

- Oil for applying on the pan

**Steps to prepare:**

- Soak the rice and lentils in fenugreek seeds for 30 minutes. Leave for the night. Drain the water and grind the mixture to a smooth paste.

- Mix in the salt and water. Then combine. Place in the refrigerator overnight. Allow it to come to room temperature before making the bread.

- Heat a small amount of oil in a pan. Then, using a large spoon, spread the batter into a thick circle. Fry until done.

# Tandalachi Bhakri (Rice Bhakri)

127

Rice Bhakri (Tandalachi Bhakri) is a Maharashtrian flatbread made from rice flour. Rice bhakri is made with only a few ingredients and is quite simple to make once you get the hang of it. Rice bhakri is best served hot, slathered with butter or ghee. Rice Flour Bhakri Recipe (Maharashtrian Tandalachi Bhakri) can be topped with Lahsun ki Chutney and raw onion on the side, or with Arhar Ki Dal with Lahsun Tadka. To make it more interesting, add some grated vegetables or greens to the dough.

**Preparation time:**20 minutes
**Cooking time:**25 minutes
**Serves:**4

## Ingredients:

- 2 cups Rice flour

- 1/2 teaspoon Salt

- Lukewarm Water, as required

## Steps to prepare:

- To start making rice flour bhakri, combine the flour and salt in a mixing bowl. Mix.

- Mix in warm water and knead to make a soft, pliable dough.

- Preheat a cast iron skillet.

- Make 2-3 portions of the dough. Make a ball out of each portion.

- Dust a flat work surface with dry flour.

- To make a thin circle, press and pat each dough ball with the palm of your hand.

- Make sure the dough does not stick to the bottom and moves freely in your hands.

- Lift the dough with both hands and place it on a hot iron griddle.

- Spread a little water on the surface of the Bhakri with your hands, then flip it over with a flat spatula.

- Cook on high heat until brown spots appear on the bottom of the Bhakri.

- Remove it from the griddle, flip it, and place it directly on the flame.

- Cook until brown spots appear or the mixture balloons up.

- To make a filling meal, serve rice flour bhakri with Lahsun ki Chutney or Arhar Ki Dal with Lahsun Tadka.

# Maharashtrian Ghavan Recipe - Rice Flour Crepes

Ghavan is a traditional breakfast recipe from Maharashtra's Konkan region that is similar to neer dosa. For a delicious breakfast, serve it with a tomato garlic chutney and a mixed vegetable korma.

Ghavan is a traditional breakfast recipe from Maharashtra's Konkan region. Traditionally, these are made with brown rice flour, a pinch of salt, jeera, and water to form a batter, and then cooked like dosas. However, because I couldn't find brown rice flour, I made it with regular rice flour.

Ghavan is comparable to neer dosa. The only difference between this and the Mangalore recipe is the type of rice used. Ghavan is a sweet recipe made with coconut and jaggery that is commonly served during festivals.

This recipe is suitable for breakfast or as a snack, and it is simple to prepare.

**Preparation time:**10 minutes
**Cooking time:**45 minutes
**Serves:**4

## Ingredients:

- 1 cup of soaked rice (soaked for 4-5 hours)

- Sunflower Oil or normal oil

- Salt as per taste

## Steps to prepare:

- 

  Grind the soaked rice for a smooth thick batter adding little water as required.

- Transfer the batter in a bowl, add salt and little water to adjust the consistency of the ghavan. Make sure its neither thick nor thin.

- Keep the batter aside for 10-15 minutes.

- Heat a non stick tawa and spread little oil. Stir the batter and pour it from the edge of the pan moving it to the center. Reduce the heat.

- Drizzle little oil from all sides and cook till its light brown. Flip onto another side and cook it.

- Serve hot with tomato garlic chutney and Tea.

# Shirvale

134

Shirvale is a traditional dish made in the Kokan villages of Maharashtra, India, with rice, ragi, or nachni (finger millet) flour and served with sweetened jaggery-flavored coconut milk. It's a time-consuming recipe. Due to the time-consuming nature of the preparation, few households in the city prepare this dish. Designed primarily for special occasions. This is an excellent dish for lactose intolerant or vegans. The tool used to make shir vale is known as "Shirvale Sacha." It is an ideal Malvani breakfast.

**Preparation time:**30 minutes
**Cooking time:**30 minutes
**Serves:**2

## Ingredients:

- 1 cup Rice flour

- 2 cups Water(Boiling hot)

- 2 tbsp Oil For Coconut milk

- 1 cup grated Coconut

- 1/4 cups grated Jaggery.(can b increased or decreased as per individual taste)

- 1/2 tsp Cardamom powder

- 1/2 tsp jeera/cumin seeds

- Salt - A pinch

## Steps to prepare:

- To make the shirvalya take a vessel add water and bring it to boil. Add salt and oil to this and let it boil for few minutes.

- Then add the rice flour, stir quickly, turn off the heat, and cover the vessels with a lid.

- Make round balls out of the mixture.

- Fill a large kadai halfway with water. Place the above rice balls in the boiling water. They will start to sink in the water. After a while, they will begin to float, indicating that they are finished.

- Put them in a sev press and press out thin noodles on a banana leaf or a greased plate while they are still hot. Repeat with the remaining rice balls.

- To make the coconut Ras, finely grind grated coconut and jeera. Pass the liquid through a strainer or cotton cloth. Remove all of the Ras from the coconut paste. Then stir in the jaggery and cardamom powder. Stir until the jaggery is completely dissolved. Soak the hot shirvalye in coconut risotto before serving. I served it with a mix veg kurma. This is how it has always been served in my family.

# Kombadi Vade Recipe

When served with chicken, Malvani Vade, also known as Wade Sagoti, becomes a world-famous dish. Tandalache Vade, also known as Malvani Rice Vade, is a Maharashtra Konkan delicacy. It is a rice and lentil mix poori that is frequently served with chicken on top. Vade Kombdi or Vade Saguti? Malvan's favourite dish is vade shaguti, also known as Kombdi vade.

Dishes are an important part of Indian culture. The diverse regions that make up this country are reflected in the food served, which includes rice dishes in South India, meat curries in North India, and various types of lentils throughout. Indian cuisine is known for the complexity of its flavours, spices, and aromas. With these simple recipes to get you started, making your own Indian dish is incredibly simple!

**Preparation time:**10 minutes
**Cooking time:**15 minutes
**Serves:**3-4

## Ingredients:

- 1 cup Rice flour

- 1/2 cup Wheat flour

- 1/2 cup Jawar flour

- 1/2 tsp. Methi powder

- 1/2 tsp. Cumin powder

- 1/4 tsp. Turmeric powder

- Salt as per taste

- 3/4 cup warm water

- Oil for frying

## Steps to prepare:

- In a dish add rice flour, wheat flour, jawar flour, methi powder, cumin powder, turmeric powder and salt. Mix it well.

- Add little warm water and knead the dough. Keep in mind the consistency of dough should be semi-soft.

- Take an aluminium foil and grease it with oil. My mother uses platic bag.

- Take a medium sized ball from the dough. Making it niceand smooth roll vada on foil with hand.

- Heat oil in a pan. When the oil is hot enough drop the vada in it.

- Press vada a little immediately after adding it. This will help vada puff up.

- When vada floats, flip it over.

- Fry both the sides till it becomes golden brown.

- Serve it with hot malvani chicken curry.